PRACTICAL &
DECORATIVE ORIGAMI

CREATIVE ORIGAMI

PRACTICAL &
DECORATIVE ORIGAMI

JAY ANSILL
PHOTOGRAPHS BY MARK HILL

CASSELL

A RUNNING HEADS BOOK

First published in the U.K.
1992 by Cassell
Villiers House
41/47 Strand
London
WC2N 5JE

PRACTICAL AND DECORATIVE ORIGAMI
was conceived and produced by
Running Heads Incorporated
55 West 21 Street
New York, New York 10010

Editor: Rose K. Phillips
Designer: Liz Trovato
Managing Editor: Jill Hamilton
Production Manager: Peter J. McCulloch

1   3   5   7   9   10   8   6   4   2

British Library Cataloguing-in-Publication Data
A catalogue record for this book is available from
the British Library.

ISBN 0-304-34147-9

Typeset by Trufont Typographers, Inc.
Colour separations by Hong Kong Scanner Craft Company, Ltd.
Printed and bound in Hong Kong by C&C Offset Printing Co. Ltd.

Dedication

To my grandfather Benjamin Ansill

Acknowledgments

One of the thrills of writing this book has been contacting folders whose names I've been familiar with for years. Everyone was extremely helpful, but I would like to single out Stephen Weiss and Samuel Randlett for their suggestions and contributions. Robert Neale has also been generous with his time and advice.

Many thanks also to Bill Masi and Roberta Tucci, who did the illustrations, and to all of the creators whose work makes up this book. The following people are due thanks for support, encouragement, inspiration, and friendship: Claudia Balant, Lillian Oppenheimer, Tony Cheng, John Montroll, Larry Cohen, Karen Berman, Laura (Riding) Jackson, Catherine Jacobs, Ellen Tepper, Robin Williamson, Pia Sundquist-Ansill, Susan Shoenfeld, Rolly Brown, and Rose K. Phillips.

Contents

Introduction

Several years ago, I was visiting Lillian Oppenheimer, founder of the Origami Center in Manhattan. There were other guests present, and we sat around a table while Ms. Oppenheimer showed us how to fold a relatively simple model. When we finished the project, a guest who had been newly indoctrinated to the world of paperfolding asked, "But what do you *do* with it?"

This query comes up more often than one might think. It is easy to question the wisdom of spending hours folding incredibly complex and detailed origami models that clutter up the bookshelves and mantelpieces of the home. Of course, many of the complex models do have a special attraction all their own and present a challenge for the patient folder, but the ones that can actually be *used* are particularly charming—especially if they don't require six fingers on each hand to make.

The projects presented in this book were chosen for both their usefulness and their beauty. Many, such as the Renaissance Shopping Bag and the Heart Gift Box, are specifically designed to function as containers. Others, such as the Tropical Flowers and the Star System, are charming room decorations. Some of the designs are traditional, yet many are recent creations. Practically all of them are simple enough that you can make them even if you've never folded a piece of paper before.

I've included a few pieces that aren't strictly origami, but are related in that they are based on principles of paperfolding. For example, folding napkins decoratively is a useful skill to dress up the table, and I've provided a few examples here though they are employed on the textile medium. The Three-D Greeting Cards are based on the "origamic architecture" pop-up cards created by Masahiro Chatani. They are a particularly delightful way to correspond; the cards also look great on a desktop in the study. Other projects are created from strips of paper or rectangles, but the results are worth bending the rules a bit.

The word origami comes from the Japanese *ori*, "to fold," and *kami*, "paper." The idea of folding paper began in China, but it wasn't until paper came to Japan that the possibilities of folding were explored more fully. Although there are traditions of paperfolding in other countries, most of the designs commonly known today come from Japan.

Since the early 1960s, largely through the tireless efforts of Lillian Oppenheimer in the United States and Robert Harbin in Britain, origami has continued to grow in popularity throughout the world. Over the past fifteen years or so, paperfolding clubs and organizations have been founded in several countries, and an impressive number of books have been written on the subject. Today, most people are familiar with this art even if they are not practitioners.

It is my hope that this book will provide an introduction to the novice paperfolder and will inspire those more experienced in origami. I wish you many happy hours of folding.

Jay Ansill
New Hope, Pennsylvania

Part I
The Basics

Paper Choices

Most art supply stores and hobby shops carry packaged origami paper. This comes in precut squares of various sizes and is coloured on one side and white on the other. Most models are well suited to this kind of paper, although brands vary in quality and some papers are not cut accurately. Accurate size is an extremely important requirement because if the dimensions are wrong, folding accurately is impossible and the finished model will look sloppy.

Often foil paper can be found. This is usually silver or gold on one side and white on the other. Although this kind of paper retains folds, any crease or wrinkle is permanent, so certain models can look sloppy if multiple folds are used to achieve the final result.

Since many of the models in this book are decorative in nature, it is a good idea to think of different kinds of paper to accent this feature. A great place to start on the search for nice paper is the giftwrap department of your stationer's shop. Wrapping paper comes in hundreds of varieties of colours, textures, and patterns and is generally easy to fold. Wallpaper can provide some interesting results, but it is important to make sure that it doesn't crack when folded. Practically anything can work. Try maps, pages from magazines and catalogues, flyers, and the like. I've even had luck folding music paper.

Sometimes it is interesting to make a model three dimensional. Two techniques that have been developed to make this possible are *wet folding* and *tissue foil*. Wet folding requires a sheet of paper that is a bit absorbent (calligraphy parchment works well), a spray bottle or bowl of water, and a cloth. During the folding process, the paper is kept slightly damp so that it can be sculpted, and the finished piece becomes stiff when dried.

Tissue foil is made by attaching a piece of tissue paper to both sides of a piece of aluminum foil with spray adhesive. The result is paper that is extremely flexible with an interesting texture. It can be sculpted to give extra character to animals. This kind of paper is great for making very complex models.

The fact that origami demands so little in the way of tools is one of the most appealing characteristics of the art form. All that is really needed is a sheet of paper. Often, the most striking result comes from an unlikely source. Be imaginative, resourceful, and adventurous, and the charm, beauty, and sheer enjoyment of origami will be revealed.

Basic Folds, Symbols, and Bases

An illustrative system of lines, dots, dashes, and arrows has been devised to make the diagrams easier to understand. Most origami books use these symbols, which constitute an international visual language. Although the diagrams that follow are self-explanatory, keep in mind the following principles:

Arrows indicate the direction of a fold.

Dots and dashes are used to indicate the folds themselves.

Dashes alone indicate a concave crease, or valley fold.

Dots alternating with dashes indicate a convex crease, or mountain fold; in this case, the paper is folded over.

Throughout the book, diagrams are shaded to indicate the coloured side of the paper should be facing outward.

Also included in this section are traditional Japanese bases. These are named for ancient models that use them as a starting point. Hundreds of contemporary models are folded from these bases. Like musical scales, they are the stepping stones to creativity and innovation. In many of the introductions to the models, the text will refer to one of these folds or bases as a starting point. Simply turn to this page to find the fold or base, and then resume with the step-by-step directions provided for the particular model.

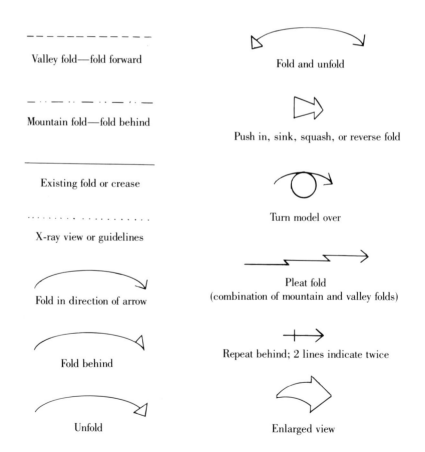

Valley fold—fold forward

Mountain fold—fold behind

Existing fold or crease

X-ray view or guidelines

Fold in direction of arrow

Fold behind

Unfold

Fold and unfold

Push in, sink, squash, or reverse fold

Turn model over

Pleat fold
(combination of mountain and valley folds)

Repeat behind; 2 lines indicate twice

Enlarged view

Preliminary Fold

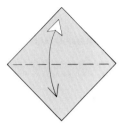

1. Fold and unfold.

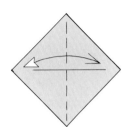

2. Fold and unfold.

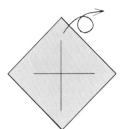

3. Turn over.

4. Fold and unfold.

5.

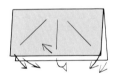

6a. Bring corners together.

6b.

1–6b.

7. Completed Preliminary Fold.

Petal Fold

1. Begin with
Preliminary Fold.

2.

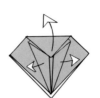

3. Unfold.

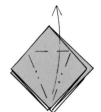

4a. Lift flap as far
as it will go.

4b.

4c.

1–4c.

5. Completed
Petal Fold.

Bird Base

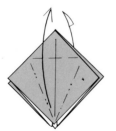

1. Petal fold;
repeat behind.

2.

3. Completed
Bird Base.

Squash Fold

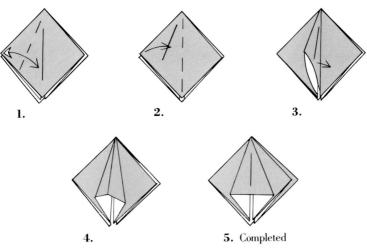

1.

2.

3.

4.

5. Completed
Squash Fold.

Rabbit Ear

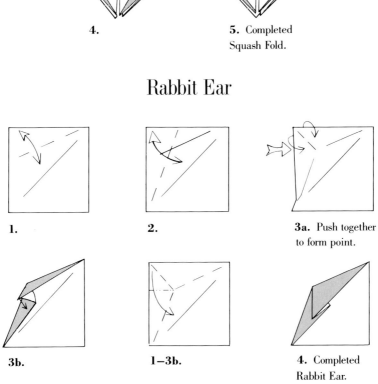

1.

2.

3a. Push together
to form point.

3b.

1–3b.

4. Completed
Rabbit Ear.

Double Rabbit Ear

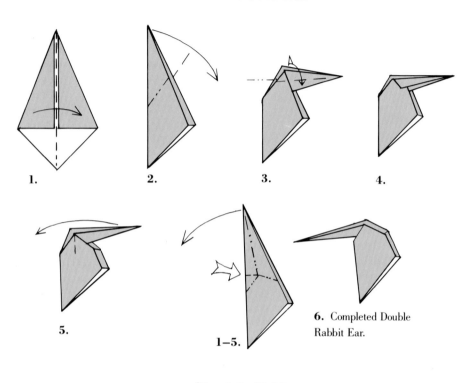

1.

2.

3.

4.

5.

1–5.

6. Completed Double Rabbit Ear.

Stretch Fold

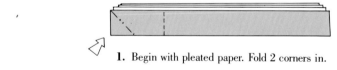

1. Begin with pleated paper. Fold 2 corners in.

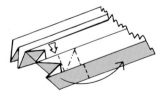

2. Pull as far as it will go.

3. Completed Stretch Fold.

Fish Base

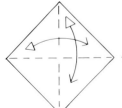

1. Fold and unfold.

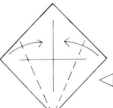

2.

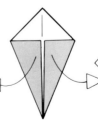

3. Unfold.

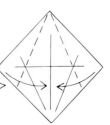

4.

5. Squash fold.

6. Squash fold.

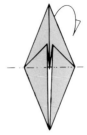

7. Fold behind.

8. Completed Fish Base.

Water Bomb Base

1. Fold and unfold.

2. Fold and unfold.

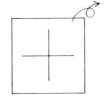

3.

4. Fold and unfold.

5.

6. Bring horizontal.

7.

8. Completed Water Bomb Base.

Reverse and Crimp Folds

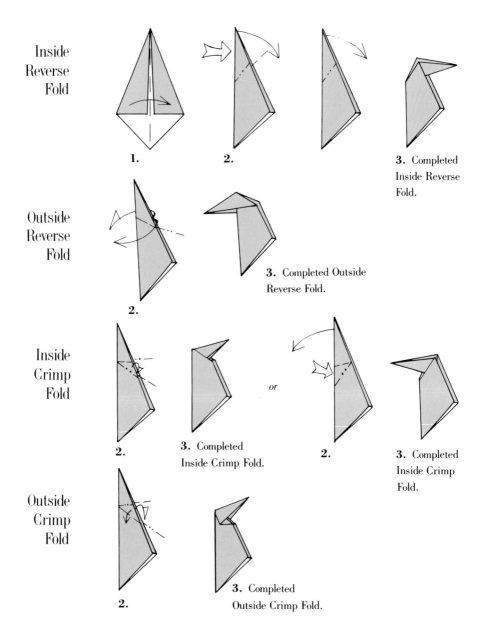

Inside Reverse Fold

1. **2.** **3.** Completed Inside Reverse Fold.

Outside Reverse Fold

2. **3.** Completed Outside Reverse Fold.

Inside Crimp Fold

2. **3.** Completed Inside Crimp Fold.

or

2. **3.** Completed Inside Crimp Fold.

Outside Crimp Fold

2. **3.** Completed Outside Crimp Fold.

Pentagon
Use a paper cutter for a clean cut.

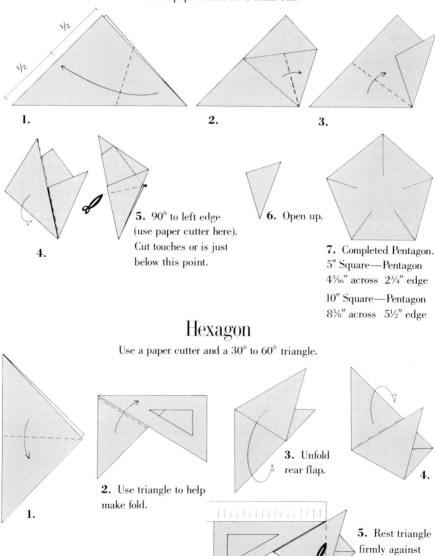

1.

2.

3.

4.

5. 90° to left edge (use paper cutter here). Cut touches or is just below this point.

6. Open up.

7. Completed Pentagon.
5″ Square—Pentagon
4³⁄₁₆″ across 2¾″ edge

10″ Square—Pentagon
8⅜″ across 5½″ edge

Hexagon
Use a paper cutter and a 30° to 60° triangle.

1.

2. Use triangle to help make fold.

3. Unfold rear flap.

4.

5. Rest triangle firmly against rule on paper cutter.

19

Part II
The Models

Everyday objects have long been a source of inspiration for craftsmen and artists. Since ancient times, urns and bowls have been embellished with decorative designs to make using them a pleasure. And such quotidian items as baskets and tableware have inspired artists to create still lifes that celebrate their simple charms. Nature is also a long-standing subject for artisans, who have represented it, particularly in the form of birds and flowers, in everything from household *objets* to sculpture.

It is from this wealth of subject matter that the models in this book were selected. The down-to-earth beauty of a well-made basket, the graceful stance of a crane, and the perfect symmetry of a star are all represented in this volume. Their beauty is captured and preserved in origami models intended to adorn and enliven the home.

The projects in this section are arranged according to level of difficulty, but novice folders shouldn't be deterred from trying some of the more complex designs. The secret is to not let yourself get frustrated, but to continue to persevere until the art of folding comes naturally and instinctively. Rated on a scale of 1 to 4, the following would apply: Napkin Rings, 1; Classic Napkin Folds, 1; Pajarita, 1; Ingenious Letter-Fold, 1; Star, 1; Crane, 2; Fancy Dish, 2; Picture Frame, 2; Renaissance Shopping Bag, 2; Perching Birds, 2 and 3; Tropical Flowers, 2 and 3; Chalice, 3; Heart Gift Box, 3; Bowl, 3; Three-D Greeting Cards, 3; and Modular Folds, 4.

Napkin Rings

These are extremely simple and beautiful models and should provide a springboard to create your own variations. Created by Catherine Abbott, they enliven any table setting and particularly lend themselves to oriental and Latin meals. Some women may even be tempted to wear them as bracelets. In the line drawings, Ring #1 refers to the narrow, brown and pink model; #2 refers to the wider, blue and pink ring, and #3 is the crested, brown-and-orange model.

Napkin Ring #1 (brown and pink)

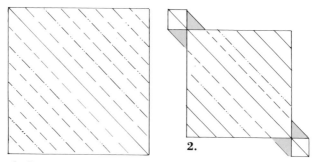

1. Precrease.

2.

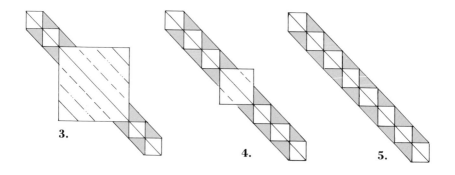

3.

4.

5.

6. Tuck one end inside the other. Completed Ring #1.

Napkin Ring #2 (blue and pink)

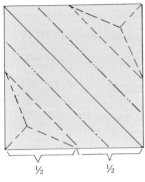

½   ½

1. Colour side facing up,
precrease and rabbit ear.

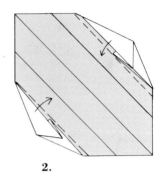

2.

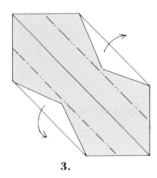

3.

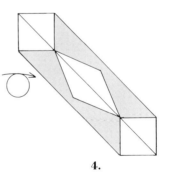

4.

5. Tuck one end inside the other.
Completed Ring #2.

Napkin Ring #3 (brown and orange)

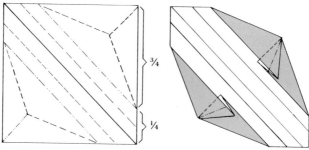

3/4

1/4

1. White side facing up, precrease then rabbit ear.

2. Squash rabbit ears.

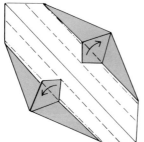

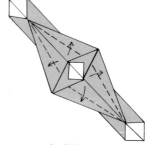

3. Valley fold, squash flaps, then accordion pleat model.

4. Valley fold top layers only. Tuck one end inside the other as in Napkin Ring #2, step 5. Completed Ring #3.

Classic Napkin Folds

Any restaurateur knows the value of the classic look of a table adorned with uniformly folded napkins. I have provided two designs for this purpose, created with ordinary table linen, not paper—unless, of course, you want to add an amusingly formal note to a children's birthday party. The Bird of Paradise is a popular fold used in many restaurants. The Shawl comes from Gay Merrill Gross, an origami artist who has a special interest in the art of napkin folding. This design looks lovely when folded from a napkin with scalloped or decorative edges.

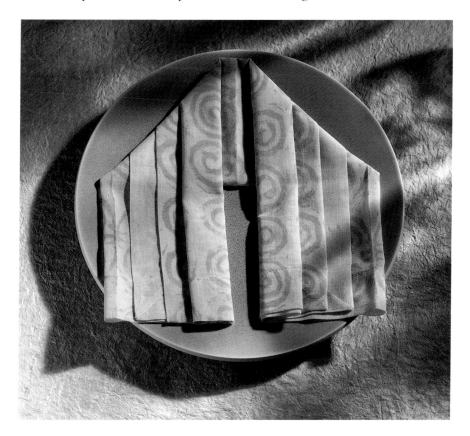

Shawl

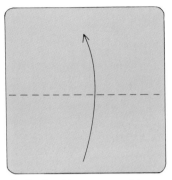

1. Begin with an open napkin. Bring the bottom edge up to around ½" below the top edge.

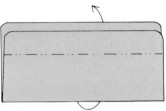

2. Fold the bottom edge behind so that it extends around 1" beyond the top edge of the napkin.

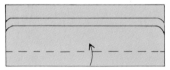

3. Fold up the bottom edge to create a hem around 1" wide.

4. The napkin now looks like this. Grasp the bottom edge and flip the napkin over so that the hem that was at the bottom is now at the back of the top edge.

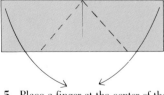

5. Place a finger at the center of the top edge and fold down each half of the top edge so that they meet at the horizontal center of the napkin.

6. Completed Shawl. If you wish, overlap the center edges slightly.

Bird of Paradise

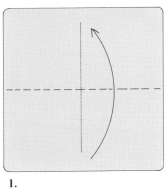

1.

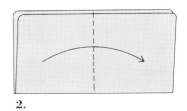

2.

3.

4.

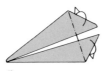

5.

6.

7.

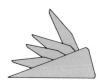

8. Completed Bird of Paradise.

Pajarita

The word *pajarita* is Spanish for "little bird." As its name implies, this design is of Spanish origin, although it is also well known throughout Britain, France, and Germany. The base of this fold can be modified into several variations, such as a pinwheel or sampan. Like the Crane, the Pajarita looks beautiful in any variety of settings. I once saw a wedding cake decorated with wildflowers, pajaritas, and cranes.

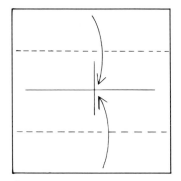

1.

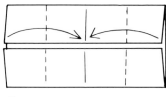

2.

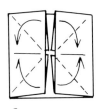

3.

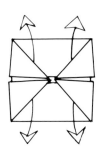

4. Pull out 4 corners.

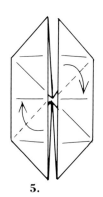

5.

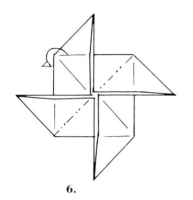

6.

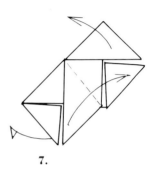

7.

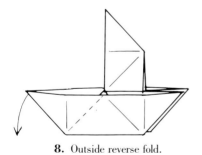

8. Outside reverse fold.

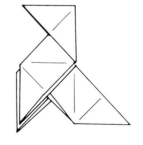

9. Completed Pajarita.

Ingenious Letter-Fold

If you wish to send a particularly special message through the mail, or want to show someone that you're thinking of them, considering making this simple combination envelope-stationery, in which the message is written directly inside the folds. A small piece of paper or flat object may also be enclosed. The envelope is perfectly suited to standard 8½-by-11-inch paper. An instant classic, this design was created by origami master Robert Neale. And it *can* travel through the mail successfully, as one was sent by myself to Neale.

Start with rectangle.

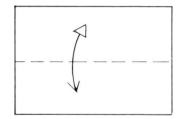

1. Valley fold and unfold.

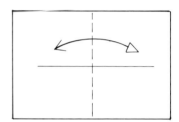

2. Valley fold and unfold.

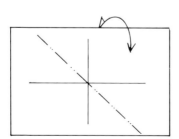

3. Mountain fold and unfold.

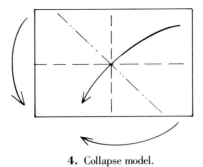

4. Collapse model.

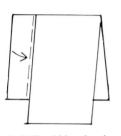

5. Valley fold and tuck into pocket. Turn over.

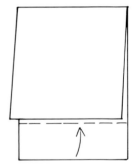

6. Valley fold and tuck into pocket.

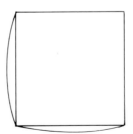

7. Completed Letter Fold.

Star

Originally developed in Germany, the Star was imported to the United States by the Pennsylvania Dutch. It makes the quintessential tree decoration and a group of them might be fashioned into a mobile. The Star is made of four strips of paper, the dimensions of which should be 1 by 24.

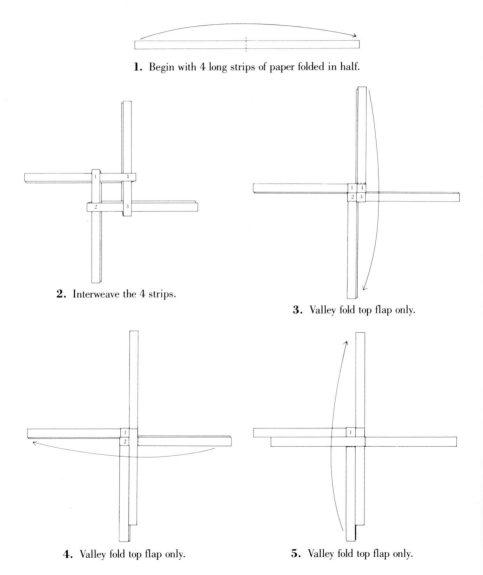

1. Begin with 4 long strips of paper folded in half.

2. Interweave the 4 strips.

3. Valley fold top flap only.

4. Valley fold top flap only.

5. Valley fold top flap only.

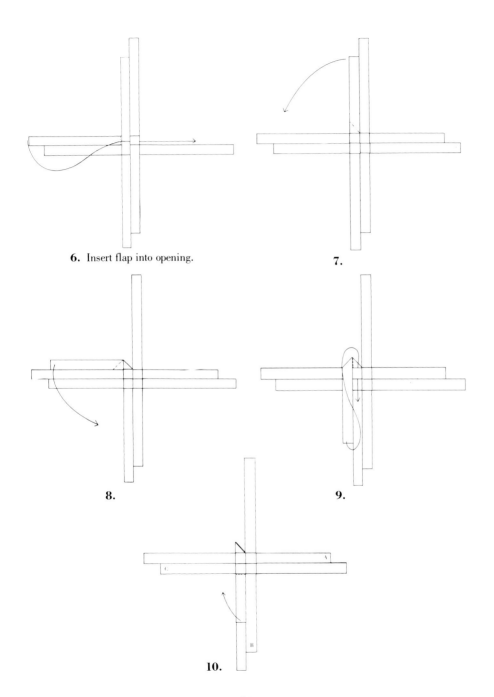

6. Insert flap into opening.

7.

8.

9.

10.

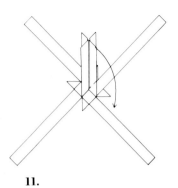

11.

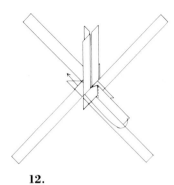

12.

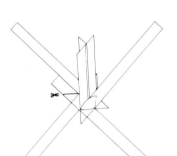

13. Cut off excess.

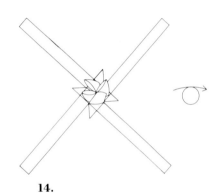

14.

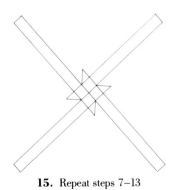

15. Repeat steps 7–13 with the other 3 flaps.

16. Completed Star.

Crane

This design is at least two hundred years old and is the most popular traditional Japanese model. It has become recognized as a symbol of peace ever since twelve-year-old Sadako Sasaki, a victim of radiation from Hiroshima, attempted to fold one thousand cranes as a gesture for universal peace. The Crane is attractive when displayed in a cabinet or on shelves, perhaps massed in groups for dramatic effect. It is also a nice addition to gift-wrapped packages. Use a 6-inch square of paper to create the design.

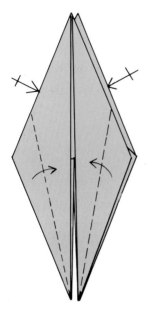

1. Begin with Bird Base.
Valley fold . Repeat behind.

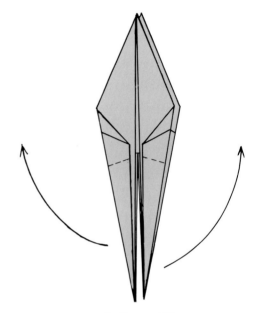

2. Reverse fold.

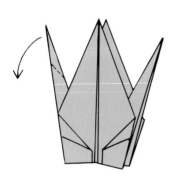

3. Reverse fold to form head.

4. Completed Crane.

Fancy Dish

Although it looks quite elegant, here is a very simple fold that has roots in both Japan and Argentina. In fact, it was one of the first models I learned how to do when I began folding as a child. Fill it with anything you wish, but be sure to display it prominently.

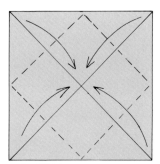

1. Fold 4 corners to center.

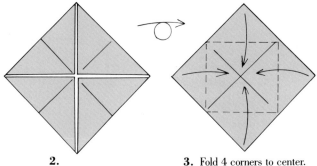

2.   **3.** Fold 4 corners to center.

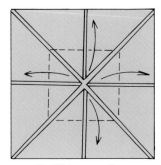

4. Fold out to edges.

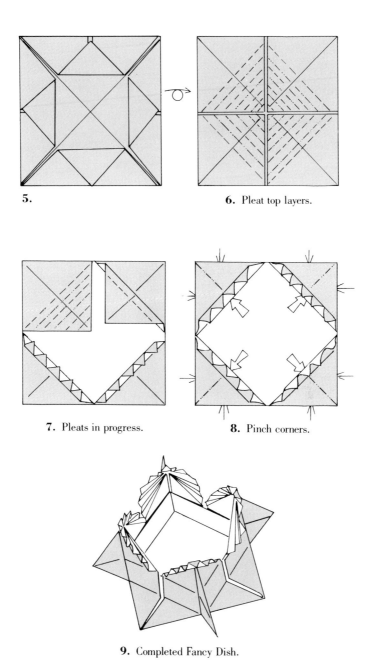

5.

6. Pleat top layers.

7. Pleats in progress.

8. Pinch corners.

9. Completed Fancy Dish.

Picture Frame

A unique way to frame a print or favorite photo is with this simple frame. Created by Aldo Putignano, it is one of his repertoire of frame designs. The print or photograph simply slips into the pocket at the center of the heart. It also has the added feature of a stand-up base to hold the photo upright. You may need to cut the photo slightly to fit the frame.

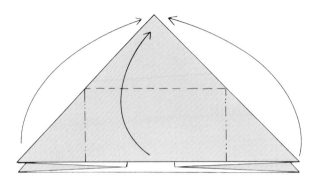

1. Begin with Water Bomb Base. Colour side up.

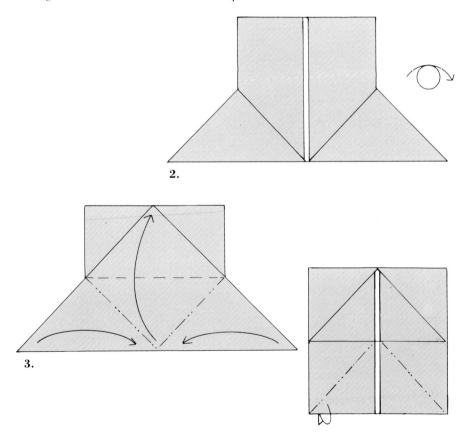

2.

3.

4. Mountain fold top layer only.

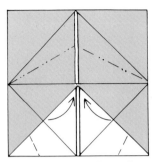

5. Lift top layer and squash.

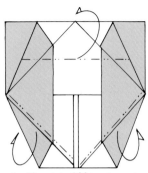

6. Mountain fold top to center. Mountain fold bottom in between layers.

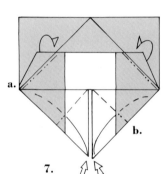

a. Mountain fold top in between layers.

b. Reverse fold.

c. Rotate 180°.

d.

7.

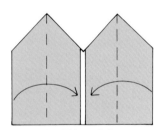

8. Valley fold single layer to center.

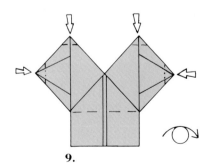

9.
a. Reverse fold all corners.
b. Valley fold slightly.

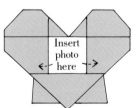

10. Insert photo. Completed Picture Frame.

Renaissance Shopping Bag

This shopping bag is a "renaissance" origami model, in that it is both beautiful and functional. To further recommend it, the bag is easy to fold and can be made from virtually any large rectangle, at least 8½ by 11 inches. Provided the paper is sturdy, it can actually carry quite a bit. To increase its usefulness, use a paper punch to add holes to the bag or add metal grommets; then attach a fancy cord for a handle. The artist who created the bag, Fred Rohm, attests to its popularity among avid shoppers. The bag, also, can be displayed in the home, perhaps filled with such decorative objects as dried flowers or marbles, or it can act as a container for gifts.

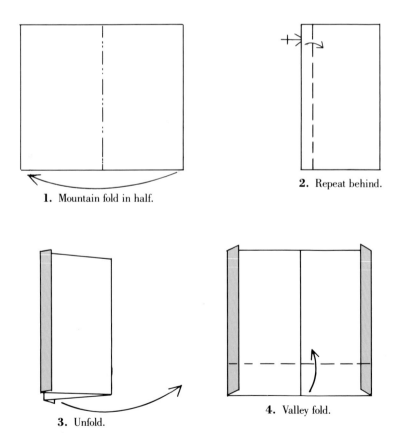

1. Mountain fold in half.

2. Repeat behind.

3. Unfold.

4. Valley fold.

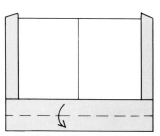

5. Valley fold and unfold.

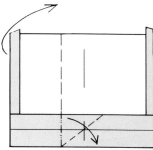

6. Swivel left side straight up so it makes a 90° angle.

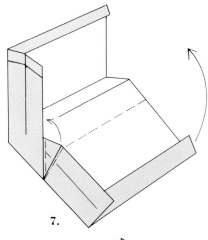

7.

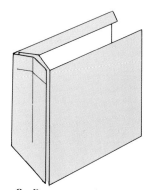

8. Repeat steps 4–7 on opposite side.

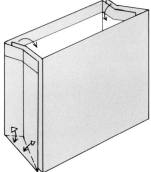

9. Fold outer lip over inner lip to lock in place. Crease sides.

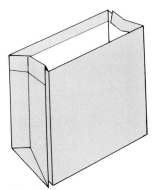

10. Completed Renaissance Shopping Bag.

Perching Birds

Referred to by one origami enthusiast as "notable for superb taste and artistry rather than for heavy-handed engineering," the work of the late Ligia Montoya is immensely appealing and elegant. Montoya, an Argentinian, pursued her own, original form of origami. It is a privilege to present this small representation of her work here. The photographs depict a parrot perched on a glass and a small swallow and a larger dove together on a roost. They can be displayed on a shelf or attached to a mobile. Birdcages have become a popular collectible for display in the home, and these origami models are also perfect ornaments for them.

Swallow

Start with Water Bomb Base.

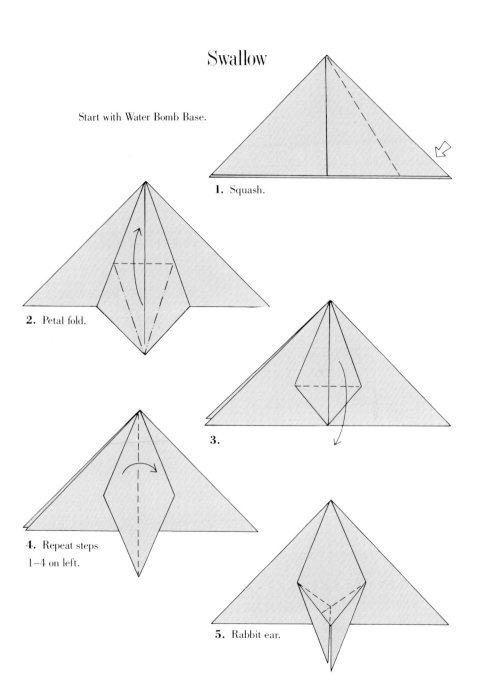

1. Squash.

2. Petal fold.

3.

4. Repeat steps
1–4 on left.

5. Rabbit ear.

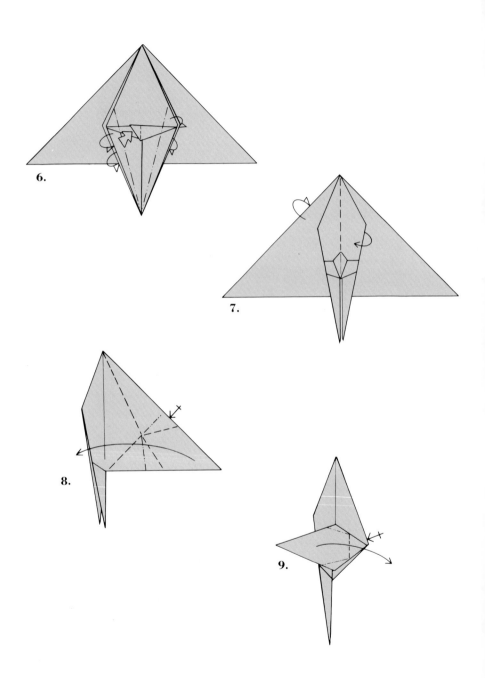

6.

7.

8.

9.

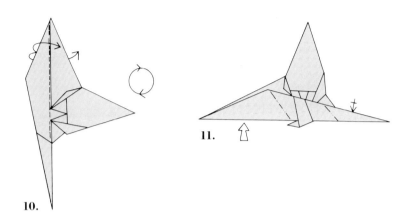

10.

11.

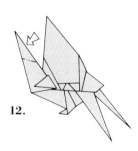

12.

12a.

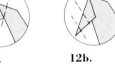

12b.

12c.

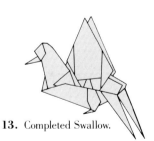

13. Completed Swallow.

Flapping Dove

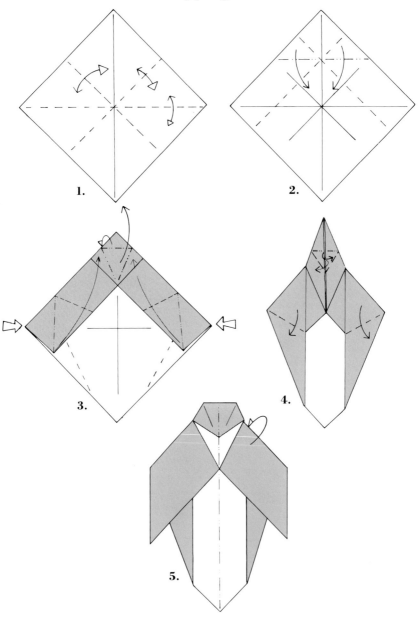

1.

2.

3.

4.

5.

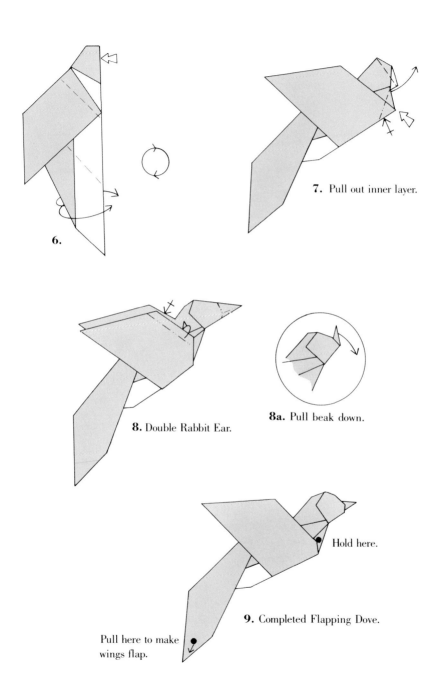

6.

7. Pull out inner layer.

8. Double Rabbit Ear.

8a. Pull beak down.

9. Completed Flapping Dove.

Hold here.

Pull here to make wings flap.

Parrot

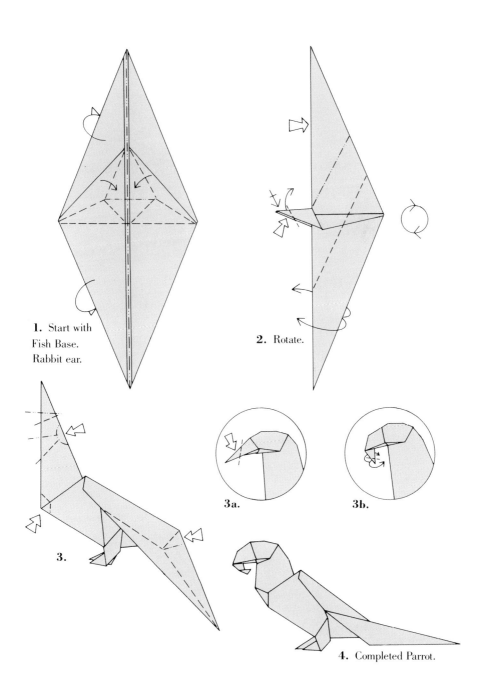

1. Start with
Fish Base.
Rabbit ear.

2. Rotate.

3a.

3b.

3.

4. Completed Parrot.

Tropical Flowers

One of the wonderful qualities of origami is its durability. When handled properly, designs can last forever. These fabulous flowers created by origami legend Ligia Montoya will never wilt and will bring beauty to rooms of your home year after year. Display them in a vase, add them to wreaths, or bundle them together with ribbon and simply display them on their sides. The photographs depict two types of flowers: a short-stemmed variety, grouped in a bowl, and a long-stemmed type, shown in a vase.

Long-stemmed Flower

Start with completed Pentagon.

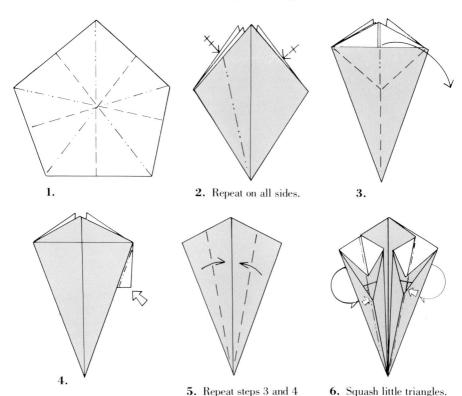

1.

2. Repeat on all sides.

3.

4.

5. Repeat steps 3 and 4 on remaining four sides.

6. Squash little triangles.

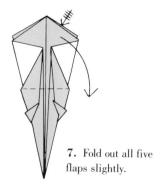

7. Fold out all five flaps slightly.

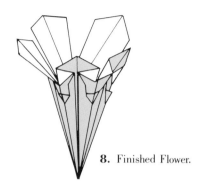

8. Finished Flower.

Short-stemmed Flower

Start with step 6 of Pentagon.

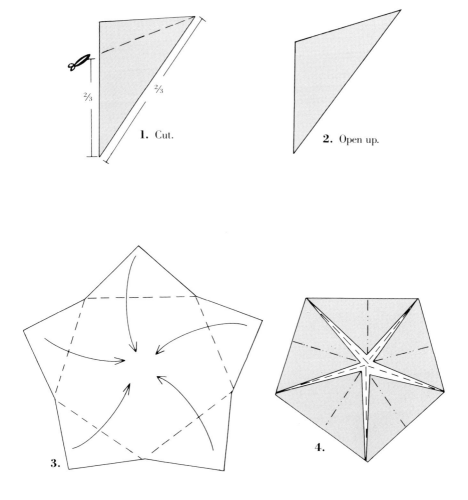

1. Cut.

2. Open up.

3.

4.

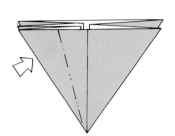

5. Squash fold.

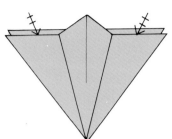

6. Repeat on remaining four sides.

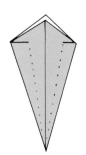

7. Squash inner flaps. Model will become 3-D.

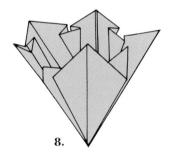

8.

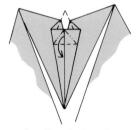

8a. Detail of inside. Petal fold all 5 points.

8b.

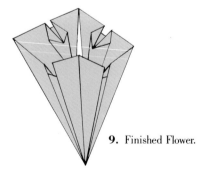

9. Finished Flower.

Chalice

This clever fold is from Samuel Randlett, a renowned champion of origami in the United States. The chalice is strikingly beautiful in itself, although it can also be filled with any number of objects—from nuts to paperclips. Randlett notes that a lid can be made to fit over the top of the cup by making the chalice from a slightly larger piece of paper.

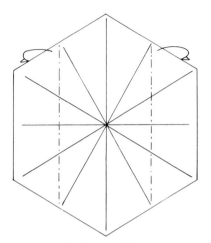

1. Mountain fold.

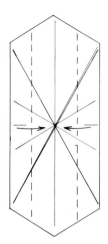

2. Valley fold.

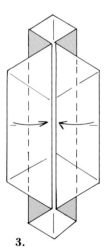

3.

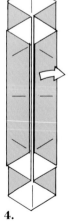

4.

Valley fold at 90°.

Unfold and repeat steps 1–4 in the other two directions.

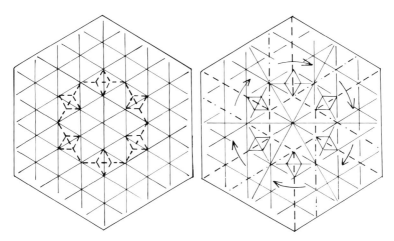

5. Form inner crease pattern.

6. Build on inner hexagon, ignoring creases made in step 5.

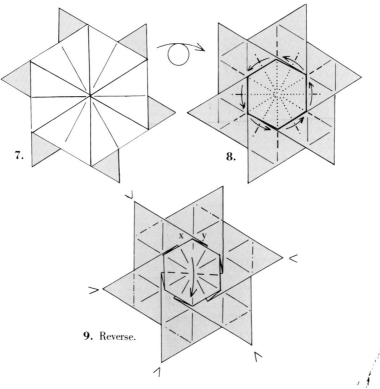

7.

8.

9. Reverse.

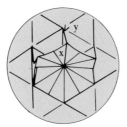

10. Squash fold on creases made in step 5.

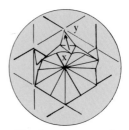

11. Return x to y and repeat 5 times.

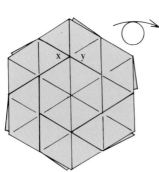

12.

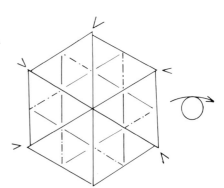

13. Reverse fold.

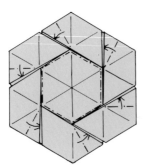

14. Tuck flaps into pockets.

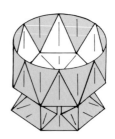

15. Completed Chalice.

Heart Gift Box

Designed by Martha Mitchen, this charming fold is based on the Heart Valentine Card by Gay Merrill Gross. It begins with any 1 by 4½ rectangle. The width of the box is equal to one half the width of the paper, and the height is one-fourth the width. Keeping these dimensions in mind, the box can be made to a specific size. Any diminutive gift would be made more special when presented inside this delightful box. It would be the perfect container for an engagement ring.

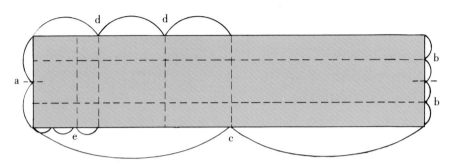

1. Fold a first, followed by b, c, d, and e.

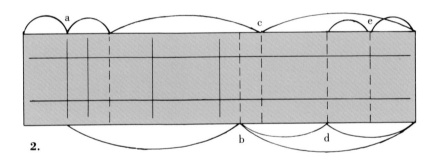

2.

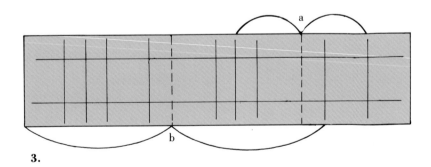

3.

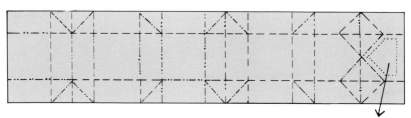

4. Insert paper slip with message: Be My Valentine xxx

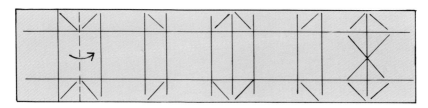

5.

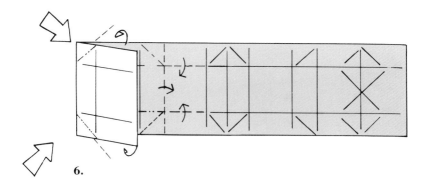

6.

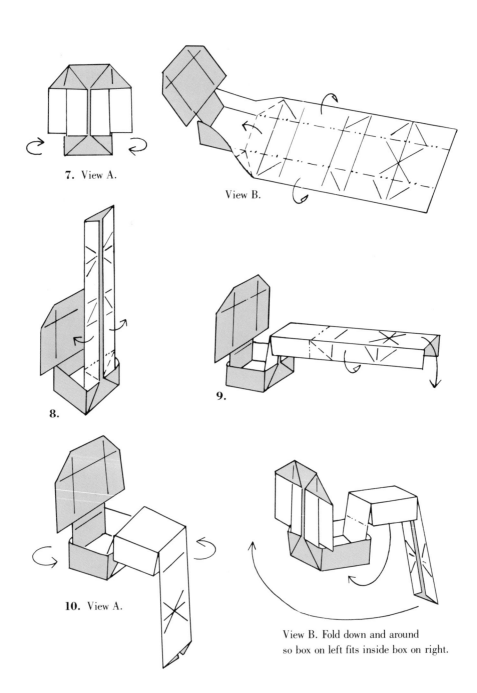

7. View A.

View B.

8.

9.

10. View A.

View B. Fold down and around
so box on left fits inside box on right.

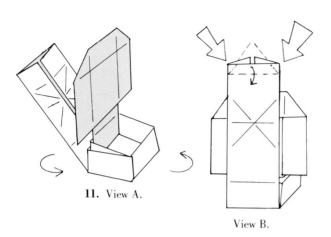

11. View A.

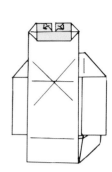

View B.

12. Crease corners.

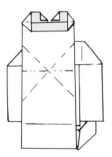

13. Fold as in water bomb base.

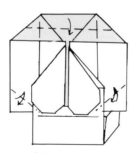

14.

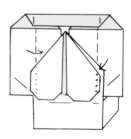

15. To lock front and back sections on top, tuck flaps into creases formed by water bomb base fold.

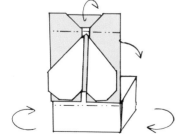

16. Fold down 90° to make flap on lid. Fold down 90° to form lid and close box.

17. Completed Heart Gift Box.

Bowl

This model makes a great centerpiece or simply a charming catch-all for anything from candies to hairbands. It is one of a number of bowls designed by Aldo Putignano. This charming model makes a lovely paper stand-in for the more expensive ceramic bowls. If you line the base with plastic or foil, it can serve as a unique container for diminutive potted plants; it is also a pretty potpourri container.

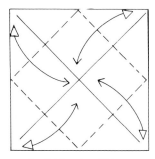

1. Fold and unfold.

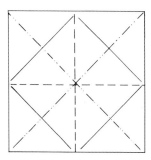

2. Make preliminary fold.

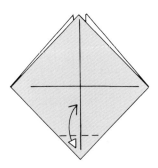

3. Fold and unfold.

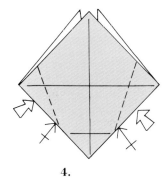

4.

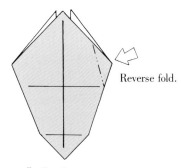

Reverse fold.

5. Top flap only.

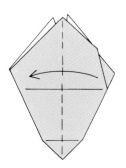

6. Top flap only.

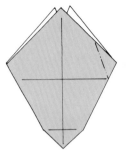

7. Repeat on remaining 3 sides.

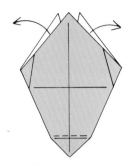

8. Open out.

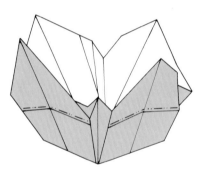

9. Fold all 4 sides inward.

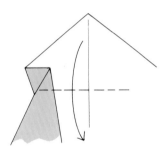

9a. Detail of inside of flap.

10. Completed Bowl.

Three-D Greeting Cards

Aside from being attractive, these "pop-up" cards are meant to encourage letter-writing in lieu of the omnipresent telephone. The cards incorporate the "dancing figure" from my personal letterhead. To make these designs, begin by photocopying this page and taping a copy over a piece of card stock. Then simply cut with a craft knife along the indicated lines. Of course, using the same principles, you can fashion your own designs. They are a perfect personal touch for holidays and other special occasions. They even have business applications—I once designed a card in this style for an architectural brochure.

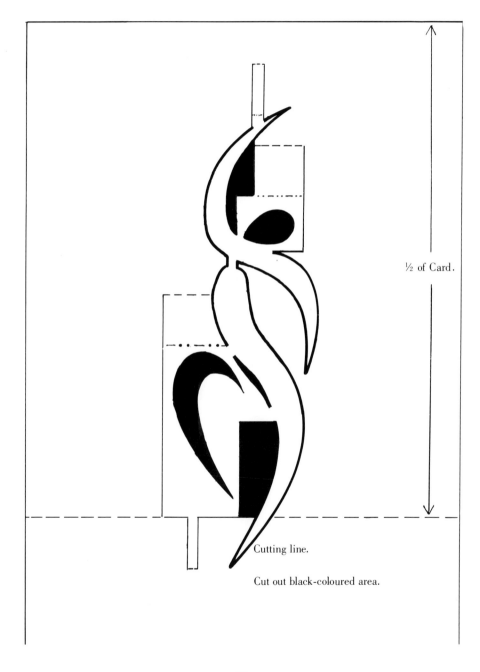

½ of Card.

Cutting line.

Cut out black-coloured area.

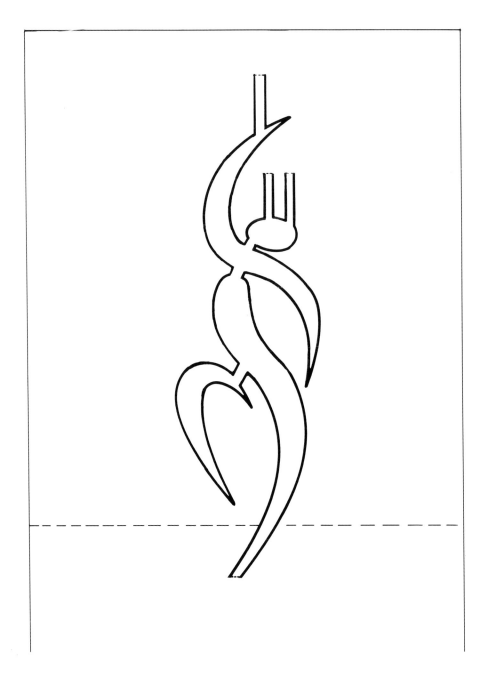

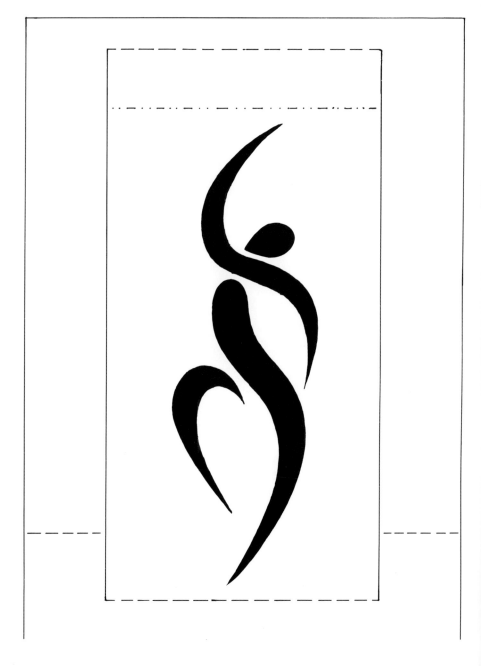

Modular Folds

These modular folds require a bit of patience to assemble, but they quickly become addictive. Strikingly sculptural, they can be displayed on tabletops or hung from the ceiling. They are especially magnificent lining the shelves of a sunlit room.

Origami artist Robert Neale calls this larger model a Star System. It is photographed here upon a table. The word "system" applies because there are so many variations and components—and so many design possibilities to explore. I have included only a few (Dr. Neale showed me several boxes filled with variations on this system). It may be helpful to use paper clips to hold the pieces together during construction.

The smaller model is called the Penultimate System and is photographed here grouped upon a desktop. It is a simple way of constructing polyhedrons. The structures are quite sturdy. It lends itself to variation and experimentation. The fact that the components fit together in a way to make the inside visible can be accentuated by placing the model near a light source or a solid background.

Penultimate System
Unit #1

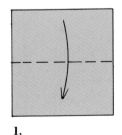

1.

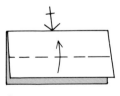

2.

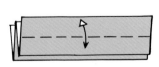

3. Fold and unfold.

4. Fold corners to meet horizontal crease.

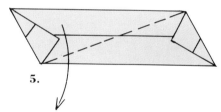

5.

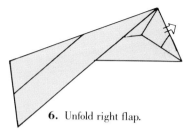

6. Unfold right flap.

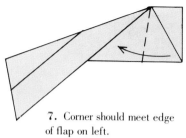

7. Corner should meet edge of flap on left.

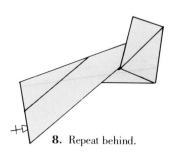

8. Repeat behind.

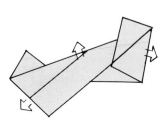

9. Open out to step 4.

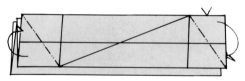

10. Reverse folds.

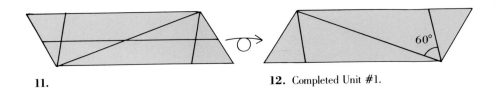

11.

12. Completed Unit #1.

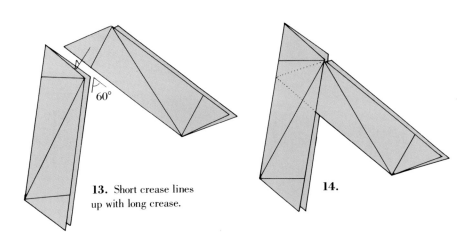

13. Short crease lines
up with long crease.

14.

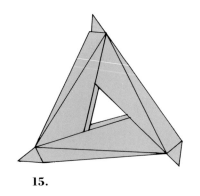

15.

6 units form a tetrahedron.
12 units form an octahedron.
30 units form an icosohedron.

Unit #2

Begin with step 4 of Unit #1.

1. Corners should meet horizontal crease.

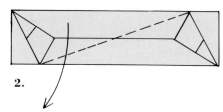

2.

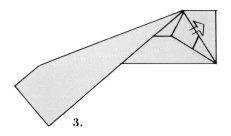

3.

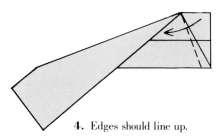

4. Edges should line up.

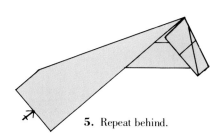

5. Repeat behind.

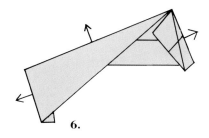

6.

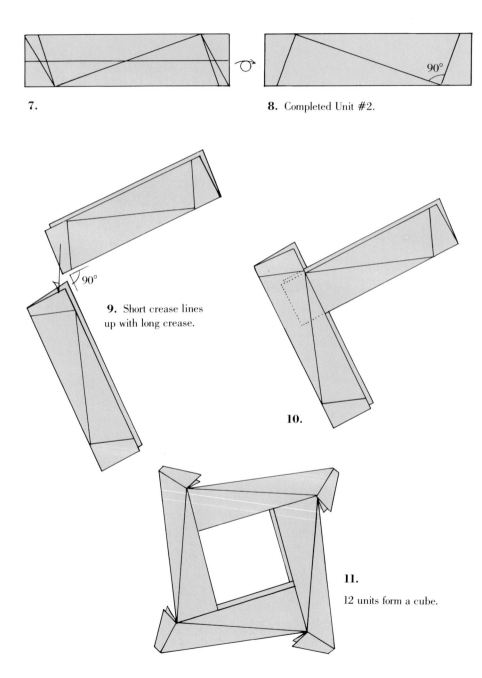

7.

8. Completed Unit #2.

9. Short crease lines up with long crease.

90°

10.

11.

12 units form a cube.

Unit #3

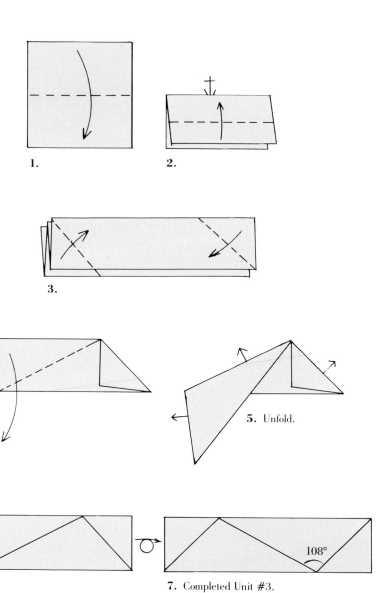

1.

2.

3.

4.

5. Unfold.

6.

7. Completed Unit #3.

108°

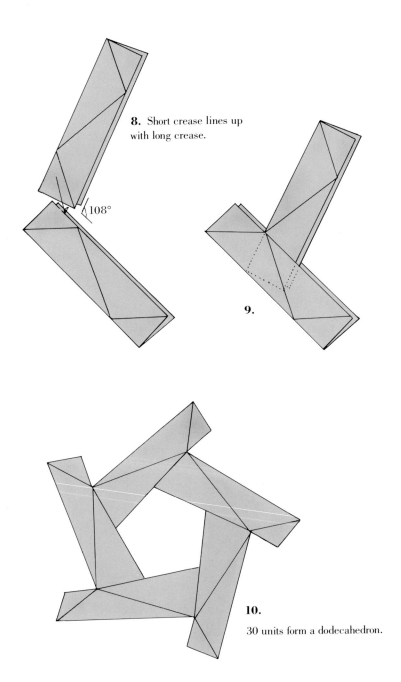

8. Short crease lines up with long crease.

108°

9.

10.

30 units form a dodecahedron.

Star System

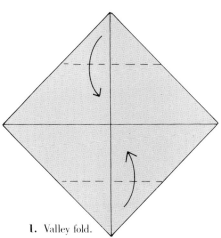

1. Valley fold.

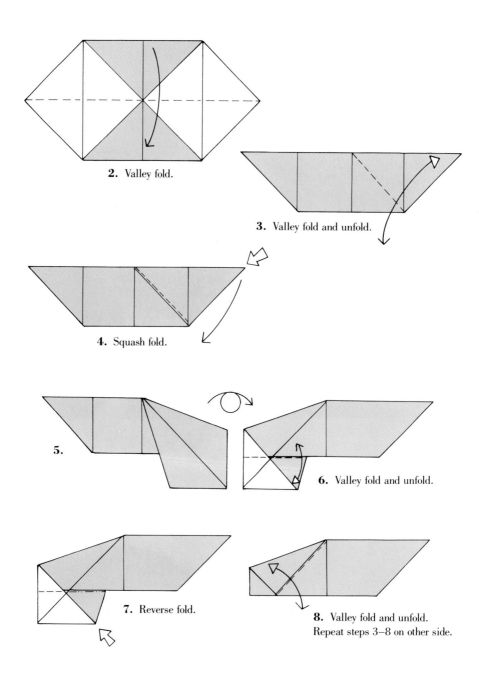

2. Valley fold.

3. Valley fold and unfold.

4. Squash fold.

5.

6. Valley fold and unfold.

7. Reverse fold.

8. Valley fold and unfold.
Repeat steps 3–8 on other side.

9. Completed Star Module.

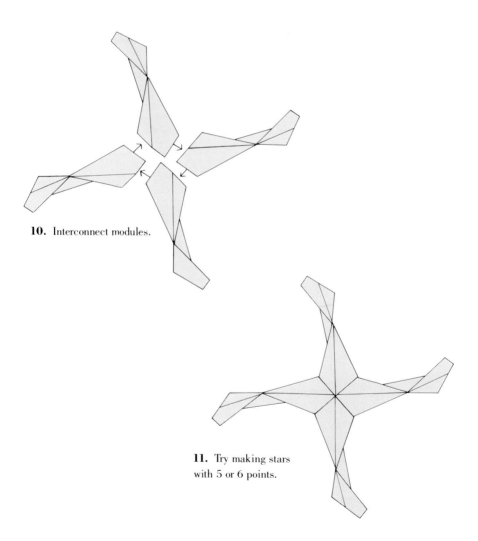

10. Interconnect modules.

11. Try making stars with 5 or 6 points.

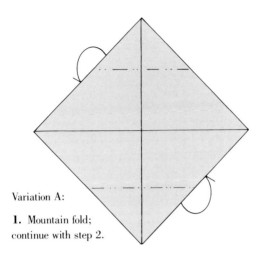

Variation A:

1. Mountain fold;
continue with step 2.

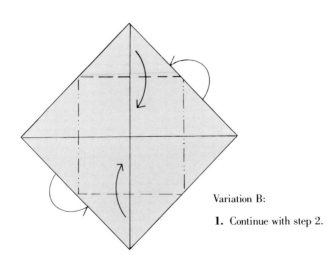

Variation B:

1. Continue with step 2.

Bibliography

Here is a list of excellent, easy-to-find origami books:

Chatani, Masahiro. *Pop-up Greeting Cards*. Tokyo: Ondori/Japan Publications, 1986.

Chatani, Masahiro. *Pop-up Paper Craft*. Tokyo: Ondori/Japan Publications, 1988.

Engel, Peter. *Folding the Universe*. New York: Vintage, 1989.

Gross, Gay Merrill. *Origami: New Ideas for Presentation*. New York: Mallard Press, 1990.

Kasahara, Kunihiko. *Creative Origami*. Tokyo: Japan Publications, 1967.

———. *Origami Omnibus*. Tokyo: Japan Publications, 1988.

Kasahara, Kunihiko, and Toshie Takahama. *Origami for the Connoisseur*. Tokyo: Japan Publications, 1987.

Kennaway, Eric. *Complete Origami*. New York: St. Martin's Press, 1987.

Lang, Robert J. *The Complete Book of Origami*. New York: Dover, 1988.

Lang, Robert J., with John Montroll. *Origami Sea Life*. Vermont: Antroll, 1990.

Lang, Robert J., with Stephen Weiss. *Origami Zoo*. New York: St. Martin's Press, 1990.

Montroll, John. *Origami for the Enthusiast*. New York: Dover, 1979.

———. *Animal Origami for the Enthusiast*. New York: Dover, 1985.

———. *Origami Sculptures*. College Park, Maryland: Antroll, 1988.

———. *Prehistoric Origami*. College Park, Maryland: Antroll, 1990.

Weiss, Stephen. *Wings and Things: Origami that Flies*. New York: St. Martin's Press, 1984.

Sources

Organizations

(Books and paper can also be ordered from origami societies. These groups are also wonderful resources for information on all aspects of paperfolding.)

The Friends of the
Origami Center of America
15 West 77 Street
Room ST-1
New York, NY 10024
(212) 769-5635

The British Origami Society
David Brill, General Secretary
253 Park Lane
Poynton, Stockport, Cheshire
SK12 1RH
United Kingdom
(0625) 8725 09

Supplies

Call or write to the following about their selection of papers produced expressly for origami and other distinctive papers that can be used for the craft.

British Origami Society
  Supplies Service
Dave and Lynn Mitchell
22 Blea Tarn Road
Kendal
Cumbria
LA9 7NA

Paperchase
213 Tottenham Court Road
London
W1P 9AS
071-580 8496

Neal Street East
7 Neal Street
Covent Garden
London
WC2H 9PU
071-240 0135

Japan Travel Centre
76 Brewer Street
London
W1R 3PH
071-437 6445

John Maxfield Ltd.
9 The Broadway
Mill Hill
London NW7
081-959 3127

Credits

The following origami creators are represented in this book:
Catherine Abbott: Napkin Rings, page 21
Jay Ansill: Three-D Greeting Cards, page 35
Gay Merrill Gross: Classic Napkin Folds, page 25
Martha Mitchen: Heart Gift Box, page 67
Ligia Montoya: Perching Birds, page 50; Tropical Flowers, page 58
Robert Neale: Ingenious Letter-Fold, page 32; Modular Folds, page 79
Aldo Putignano: Picture Frame, page 44; Bowl, page 72
Samuel Randlett: Chalice, page 6.3
Fred Rohm: Renaissance Shopping Bag, page 47